Cheap

OTHER BOOKS BY RUTH STONE

In an Iridescent Time
Topography and Other Poems

Cheap

NEW POEMS AND BALLADS

Ruth Stone

Harcourt Brace Jovanovich

New York and London

For the countless women I respect and admire;
and especially, Marcia Stone Croll, Phoebe Stone,
and Blue Jay Stone, my incomparable daughters

Printed in the United States of America

Some of these poems appeared previously in Boston Arts Review,
California Quarterly, The Iowa Review, and Modine Gunch
Anthology.

Library of Congress Cataloging in Publication Data
Stone, Ruth.
   Cheap: new poems and ballads.

   I. Title.
PS3537.T6817C5   811'.5'4   75-9555
ISBN 0-15-117034-7
ISBN 0-15-616798-0 (pbk.)

B C D E

Contents

Bargain

I was not ready for this world
Nor will I ever be.
But came an infant periled
By my mother sea,
And crying piteously.

Before my father's sword,
His heavy voice of thunder,
His cloud hung fiery eyes,
I ran, a living blunder.

After the hawker's cries,
Desiring to be shared
I hid among the flies.

Myself became the fruit and vender.
I began to sing.
Mocking the caged birds
I made my offering.

"Sweet cream and curds . . .
Who will have me,
Who will have me?"
And close upon my words,
"I will," said poverty.

II

Cheap

Not knowing I wasn't free
I would slam the door
Of his rented hacienda.
He was young and cheap;
Sweet smelling sweat.
I was easy in my sleep;
Gathered my hair
In a simple plait;
Not fretting myself.
And surely as sun up
He would follow me
From century plant
To lemon tree,
Over succulents and thorns,
Down to the stretching sand,
To the naked hiss,
Where he'd catch my hand
And we'd run blind as moles
With supple skins
Rubbing together like skeins
Of trader's silk;
Braying, galloping
Like a pair of mules.

Sabbatical Love

Living in Selsey was like living in sin.
In the morning Mrs. Harmsworth came puffing
On her bicycle to tidy up. Dangerously red and purple,
Her veins. The wind in her.
The terrible story of her chilblains.
How you hated to give the gardener
His one pound six on Thursday
When he stood waiting at our door
With a wretched bouquet clipped from the mangy annuals,
"For her," waving it toward me.
How like the garden he was; those reproachful mounds
Of swollen marrows turning to slush,
The rich slime of the parsley bed.
Lover-like we sneaked away to walk on the shingle;
Leaving our neglected daughters in a playroom
Overlooking some faintly ominous shrubbery.
Were those puffins, galanules, awks,
Crying around the muddy estuary? Where, in our middle-aged
    madness,
We climbed out over deep water
On piles and planks that had rotted in the continuous spray.

Codicil

I am still bitter about the last place we stayed.
The bed was really too small for both of us.
In that same rooming house
Walls were lined with filing cases,
Drawers of bird's eggs packed in cotton.
The landlady described them.
As widow of the ornithologist,
Actually he was a postal clerk,
She was proprietor of the remains.
Had accompanied him on his holidays
Collecting eggs. Yes,
He would send her up the tree
And when she faltered he would shout,
"Put it in your mouth. Put it in your mouth."
It was nasty, she said,
Closing a drawer with her knee.
Faintly blue, freckled, mauve, taupe,
Chalk white eggs.
As we turned the second flight of stairs
Toward a mattress unfit for two,
Her voice would echo up the well,
Something about an electric kettle
At the foot of our bed.
Eggs, eggs, eggs in secret muted shapes in my head;
Hundreds of unborn wizened eggs.
I think about them when I think of you.

Loss

I hid sometimes in the closet among my own clothes.
It was no use. The pain would wake me
Or like a needle it would stitch its way into my dreams.
Wherever I turned
I saw its eyes looking out of the eyes of strangers.
In the night I would walk from room to room slowly
Like an old person in a convalescent home.
I would stare at the cornices, the dull arrangements of furniture.
It all remained the same.
It was not even a painting.
It was objects in space without any aura. No meaning attached.
Their very existence was a burden to me.
And I would go back to my bed whimpering.

From the Other Side

Maurice, had I known about salvation in art,
Child of pleasure, the affirmative,
While I swung from the monkey tree,
Would you have loved me more or less?
My metaphor, my suspect,
In pale recollection, apart from the elegance of your feet,
The truths of suffering return to me.

Gesture of open palms;
Your hands; your long fingers
Which were like rain on the western slopes.
I am disguised and travel with strangers.
I had no proofs of endings or beginnings.
In my simple animal,
Sleeping and waking were familiars of birth and death.
To wrap myself in your bony arms
Was the revelation of mortality.

Maurice, I seek salvation that is not there.
The measure of suffering is the knowledge of pleasure.
Consider the infinite anguish of this insanity;
Only in the impossible are we transformed to artifact.

The Tree

I was a child when you married me,
A child I was when I married you.
But I was a regular mid-west child,
And you were a Jew.

My mother needled my father cold,
My father gambled his weekly gold,
And I stayed young in my mind, though old,
As your regular children do.

I didn't rah and I hardly raved.
I loved my pa while my mother slaved,
And it rubbed me raw how she scrimped and saved
When I was so new.

Then you took me in with your bony knees,
And it wasn't them that I wanted to please—
It was Jesus Christ that I had to squeeze;
Oh, glorious you.

Life in the dead sprang up in me,
I walked the waves of the salty sea,
I wept for my mother in Galilee,
My ardent Jew.

Love and touch and unity.
Parting and joining; the trinity
Was flesh, the mind and the will to be.
The world grew through me like a tree.

Flesh was the citadel but Rome
Was right as rain. From my humble home
I walked to the scaffold of pain, and the dome
Of heaven wept for her sensual son
Whom the Romans slew.

Was it I who was old when you hung, my Jew?
I shuffled and snuffled and whined for you.
And the child climbed up where the dead tree grew
And slowly died while she wept for you.

Goyim wept for the beautiful Jew.

Becoming You

I think about territory
And how you invaded my skin.
Now, I shall grow
Until I encompass you.
There in your box,
Barefoot in your best suit,
The rocks grind little nudges in the plate.
The lightning runs along the ground
Until, unable to stay apart
It pulls down blood from the cloud.
Shudders us both.
With my feet tapping the walks between us
I am everywhere growing larger
And my dimensions now include
Your perfectly clear pattern;
Every crystal molecule and deviant particle
Available to my pseudopods
As, taking my time,
I come on digesting you.

Habit

Every day I dig you up
And wipe off the rime
And look at you.
You are my joke,
My poem.
Your eyelids pull back from their sockets.
Your mouth mildews in scallops.
Worm filaments sprout from the pockets
Of your good suit.
I hold your sleeves in my arms;
Your waist drops a little putrid flesh.
I show you my old shy breasts.

The Innocent

I remember you
As a porcupine is remembered for its quills
But forgotten in a dream of forgetting
As pain falls away into no pain.

I remember you
As a tree cut by the saw
Comes down into the snow on the mountain.

I remember you
In breaths of air turned white,
As men like demons breathing fire
Chained logs.

I remember you
In the sound of an oak stake
Hammered into the frozen heart of the ground.

III

Mist at the University of Illinois

Bird sounds tacking tree to tree;
A space of lifting mist peels to drab
Drugstores, bookstores, on an old-fashioned street;
Gabled rooming houses gray as Inland steel.
Plain flat town cluttering its eaves and chimneys
In the severe business of sparrows.

Here I am on the campus where we met;
By the math building, near the gym where you showered
When you had no money for rent.
Your long arms, your long narrow fingers,
Always restless; your mind always too brilliant.
I stand by a dead elm that has been buttressed, cement
Imbedded in the stretched-apart double trunk.
Prepared with paved knowledge of your absolute disappearance
From the college of my dreams; bells
Beat out explicit hours. Pigeons coax the same as then.

In warm weather we went sometimes to look at the Percherons
In their stanchions on the South Farms;
Their big outmoded bodies, their incongruous feathered fetlocks
Stamping in the acid piles of dung. And the bulls,
Laced in thick wooden slats through which we stared uneasily
While they stood larger than life, placid amid the slough of stale
    urine,
Their testicles hanging like the threat of lightning
Under their narrow haunches. Clouds moving up from the moody
    west
Bearing down upon us, oppressive as the prairie stretched dark
    to the rim
Smelling of pig slop and blood. We were sometimes carried out
    of ourselves
By a long semaphore of freight cars leaning and rumbling.

Someone, oriental jet black hair rising with each step forward
Like seaweed in ocean swell, passes me in the mist.
Trees secretly upside down unravel their roots in the dragging air.
Aimless, without history, I crawl with the slugs in the ooze.

Illinois

Close up, shaved hay fields,
Corn stubble.
The horizon spins out flat.
Aluminum silo blinking in the sun.
Birds and gnats
Funnel up
Shading into tornados
Dancing along the edge of nowhere.
At your feet
Awkward sprays of chickory,
Blooming late;
Blue as imagined spaces,
Blue as a young pig's eyes.

Detail for a Letter

Is it that I no longer write poems,
Substituting hasty messages?
Passing the discarded candy wrapper
In the tame monkey's yard,
The empty box of Kellogg's Smacks, so poignant,
Caught in the barberry bushes;
I see, approaching from an infinite distance,
A former student drinking a bottle of strawberry soda.
He lifts it to his lips like a flute.
A long low ridge of variegated leaves
Has been raked and is now being scattered by the wind.
All day yesterday it misted, it rained.
The intolerable heat oozed into the gutters.
Unable to write poems any more,
I pin up messages to you in my head.
The gray, the white, the brown, the green, the pink houses,
Almost all of them come up between clumps of hydrangeas
And some of them have porch swings, chrysanthemums in faded
    urns.
Slowly, slowly the dog and I chained to one another
Pass lawns and fences, gravel driveways.
The street shudders with cars that move like schools of fish.
The postman, making an early delivery, goes at a steady pace;
His leather bag riding his hip, helping the earth turn.

Prairie Tanker

Under the storm clouds
Headlights of a milk tanker
Over the man-made rise;
Buffeting air it crosses
The concrete bridge accompanied,
As an incoming ship,
With birds wheeling above
The diesel stack.
Moving together, undulating like a pulse,
The starlings claim their territory;
Escort the tanker past fields
Whose furrows are ploughed to the horizon.

Fading

As though approaching a mirror,
The post office recedes
To an unreal building in my mind.
I climb the public steps,
My former lightness inside clothes
Amazed at itself.
On the same shelf similar letters
Edged red and blue.
Encephalograms of difficult birth,
Butchered umbilical cords.
The same gray postal clerk
Moving more slowly by the minute.
The same squat provincial town
Dividing in hunks of cement.
I mail no letter to you,
Send no cry through the air
To fade out of time
As bending light.

Tic Tac Toe

Someone is never done with laying out streets.
Old women looking out of windows
Rap sharp warnings to dogs on leashes
Taking liberties with boxwoods.
People at the other ends of leashes
Think seriously of making parallel lines meet
And sigh inside their heads,
Pulling in their stomachs and promising
To exercise more, drink less, grow brilliant.

Room

Someone in the next apartment
Walks slowly back to a room abutting mine.
I am on this side, sitting.
It is uncomfortable trying to be quiet.
For weeks coming in here to change my clothes,
I think, are my clothes too daring?
And the sound of water rushing in
Filling a tub in the other room
Makes a loud continuity,
As though many people might be living here,
Twining their arms about me,
Passing me in the hall,
Making tender jokes.
Sunlight enters the room near the ceiling.
And shadows of leaves letting go
Flash in downward slants
Falling inside the room
To sink through the floor.
And I think
Is this the way it will be?
And I listen
With my ear against the plaster.

Obscene Phone Calls

Rabid fox and mangy rabbit.
Outside, back and forth a string of abalone shells
Swings in the wind,
Stutters the noon-blind snow
Dirty where it fell
Out of a dirty sky.
I am here behind the window
Waiting for your voice again.
I look out of this long animal cell.
The potted ivy curls, fingering up.
In a far room in my memory the phone rings.
It is you, breathing,
Rolling in beer flesh,
Breaking out of your undies in damp emotion,
Padding barefoot through the shag;
Your bath going down the drain in huge swallows.
Bird feathers puff gray on the grass.
Breast feathers, tail feathers, russet tipped,
Tangled in fences,
Singing louder than the sparrows.
It begins to rain.

U of My

When my dog barks and we go for a walk
I say to him, "avuncular, attaché, Williamsburg!"
And he pees on the evergreens.
"Horseradish," my cat cries after dark,
"Out, out." It is the fault
Of the university, of course,
That we live over the drying rooms;
That the laundry machines belch all night.
Recently an entire population of ants
Crept out of the geraniums
And is climbing the plaster.
Soon, I think, they will starve to death
Like those unfortunate people living
On lateritic soils, for these walls
Will not give up any nutrients.
I speak for them, "help, help!
Gestalt, Gestalt! University!
University of my dreams."

Dream of Wild Birds

Sweat curls off the lake the color of ochre.
The lead flamingo leaps flapping and dancing,
His neck contorted. He clicks his beak.
The water becomes blue-green. The sun rises.
This is a movie, a film, a picture, a little frame.
His bones, bathed in bird's blood, shine through
The x-ray. His is an elegant skeleton.
His feathers, like the clouds, outlined with light,
Spreading, shaking. The wind coming in a thick current
Pulling loose down from his breast and whirling it
Up, up. It is a passion of light.
At once in slow motion the entire flock
Dances in pink ballet tutu, awkward grace, up and down,
Bowing and clicking. Meanwhile, the ovum is swelling
And the sperm is growing agitated. The time for leaving
The dark blood has come and the flagella lash against
The hot walls. The sun and the gnats burn over the lake
Catching fire in the feathers of the flamingos,
And the sun rises higher and higher.

Vegetables I

In the vegetable department
The eggplants lay in bruised disorder;
Gleaming, almost black,
Their skins oiled and bitter;
A mutilated stem twisting
From each swollen purple body
Where it had hung pendulous
From the parent.
They were almost the size
Of human heads, decapitated.
A fingernail tearing the skin
Disclosed pith, green white,
Utterly drained of blood.
Inside each skull, pulp;
Close packed, dry and coarse.
As though the fontanels
Had ossified too soon.
Some of these seemed to be smiling
In a shy embarrassed manner,
Jostling among themselves.

Vegetables II

Saturated in the room
The ravaged curry and white wine
Tilt on the sink.
Tomatoes in plastic bag
Send up odors of resentment,
Rotting quietly.
It is the cutting room, the kitchen,
Where I go like an addict
To eat of death.
The eggplant is silent.
We put our heads together.
You are so smooth and cool and purple,
I say. Which of us will it be?

Periphery

You are not wanted
I said to the older body
Who was listening near the cupboards.
But outside on the porch
They were all eating.
The body dared not
Put its fingers in its mouth.
Behave, I whispered,
You have a wart on your cheek
And everyone knows you drink.
But that's all right, I relented,
It isn't generally known
How clever you are.
I know you aren't appreciated.
The body hunted for something good to eat,
But the food had all been eaten by the others.
They laughed together carelessly outside the kitchen.
The body hid in the pantry near the refrigerator.
After a while it laughed, too.
It listened to all the jokes and it laughed.

Separate

I want to tell you something with my hands.
I have been weeding the garden.
Many young people come here
Playing drums, picking strings,
Holding their wooden hearts.
The radishes are strong and pithy;
The lettuce is bolting.
The leaves of the radishes are jagged like knives.
These young people encamp around their instruments
As though they are around a fire.
They watch for the signal.
It passes between them.
Sometimes I water the toads
Who wait for insects under the zucchini leaves.
Indian bedspreads are not as gorgeous
As the muted patterns of toads.
Sometimes I lift a green lacewing
Out of a trough of water
And it stretches up like a cloud
Filling the universe with a gauze torque.
I want to tell you something with my fingers.
The space between us is a crack in the ice
Where light filters green to blue
Deeper than the fissures of continents.
All of time stretched like a web between
Was sucked into that space.
I want to tell you something with my hands,
My enormous hands which lie across a broken mirror
Reflected in broken pieces of themselves.

As Now

In times of the most extreme symbols
The walls are very thin,
Almost transparent.
Space is accordion pleated;
Distance changes.
But also, the gut becomes one dimensional
And we starve.

V

Overlapping Edges

Starlings flock to roost across rubble of shocked corn,
Last summer's scattered bone stalks ready to be ploughed under;
As though we were dismembered, as though we were in an open
    grave.
A veil of powdered limestone is suspended.
It is the fertilizer man in the corn field.
In the open pits of Auschwitz, scattered thigh bones, matchstick
    arms.
Through veils of limestone at the far edge,
Tombs of highrise apartments, silent, without lament.
And starlings, generations of birds puzzling along the windrows.

Westhaven

Along the swamp falling sycamore leaves
Make red stars in the rushes and snakeskins,
Caught on fences, flutter like Chinese flags.
Exploding seeds parachuting up, sail struck with light.
Everything splits and lets go. The sky lifts
Higher and higher over the first hill.

It is the way light falls; angles breaking into haloes
Around bronze tussets; tinctured yellow toward the footpath
Over the spillway. Single blue late chickory and bone white
Queen Anne's lace, composite; repeating over the meadow.

To lie against the hill waiting for voices
To catch up with you; the smell of the sweet drying grass;
Hearing among the other voices
The delayed imperative buzzing out of the weeds,
The big-eyed grasshopper rubbing his legs for love.

Balance

Sprays of fine needles
In Sumi brush strokes.
What million legs and wings
Rub the upwashing heated air
Through the white pines.
Laced everywhere with foster daughters,
Pale green maples twisting up
In the stiff arms of pines,
The forest sighs in its millennium.
Cedars, old mandarins,
Venerable with incense,
Their sparse beards symbolizing
A fragile balance.
Underfoot,
The wild strawberry leaves;
Separate, barely flourishing.
Gray creeping lichens
Spreading over the alluvial clay soil,
Lightly.

Remembering

Somewhere on the path by your house
The brook is covered with yellow leaves.
An empty wine bottle, like a still life,
Balances on a weathered table. The lawn chairs
Wait for snow to buttress their sagging joints.
Remembering the way Monarch butterflies
Would zig-zag between the milkweed flowers,
I am drunk on the emptiness of being not there.

Beginning to Live

I'm beginning to understand that man in old boots
Who sits on his front porch looking at the wood pile;
A bottle of booze behind his wash basin.
He is waiting for snow.
In the wet air crows and bluejays set up a rollick
And try for the sun. But the heifers, grazing through November,
Slog in the sticky clay, their cloven marks filling up
With rain among the moonstone mushrooms.
Those women who gathered squaw-wood, their eyes
Were not clear. They were red rimmed, smoke irritated;
But stoic from looking at the brown quiet of fallen pine needles.
Sitting here saying things to myself, the long staccato drill
Of leg-rubbing insects stops for a moment when the rain begins.
A leaf imitating a dying butterfly falls in reluctant spirals.
I will sit here drinking until it snows and then
I'll go in and build a fire.

The Late Comers

Late for the harvest,
Our overseer is the wind
That hides in the crevice.
It is the echo of too much
Scattered in haste.
"Save me," cries the meteor,
Bursting into flame.
Corn holds out half-ripe fingers
And begins to whisper.
Willows bend like ostrich fans
Held by insincere ladies.
"Tell us," cry the bugs,
Crawling around on the wrinkled ground,
"Is there nothing more to eat than this?
We want to split and cast our old skins."
Constellations flash.
Single crystals of ice sweat and multiply.
The cicadas complain in the wheat stubble,
"Where are we? Where are we?"

Path

It was an old path.
It went uphill through the woods.
You led the way because you were the youngest.
"It's my path," you said.
Yes, these paths always belong to someone.
They criss-cross through my mind,
The leaves smelling like campfire sweetness,
The dogs diverging in the underbrush.
But the woods; going up so straight and thin,
Leaves beginning to turn,
The shadows soothing, saying,
"Let us drift easy and lie down together.
Never go away, but lie here under this bush."

Communion

Birds circle above the hay barn.
A young bull gets up from the mud;
The tuft under his belly like a clump of grass.
He bellows; his curly throat stretched up,
His head half turned yearning upward from the wood slatted pen
Where he sleeps or tramples the sloughed manure.
The birds gather to cheep in unison.
A row of oak trees shining like waxed veneer
Ranges down wind-break.
The sky, vague blue behind a gauzy cumulus;
Pale fall sunlight glazes the barn shingles.
Now a chorus of bulls forcing music out of their bodies,
Begins and begins in terrible earnestness.
And the birds, undulating and rising, circle
And scatter over the fall plowed strips.
What they are saying is out of their separateness.
This is the way it is. This is the way it is.

Bird Tree

The tree is clotted with dickcissels, mourning doves.
Leaves scatter with the flock.
Here at the edge of a suburb, oaks
Form medieval walls against the city.
The tree, comfortably frowzy,
Stretches through early mist.
A continual order of conversation
Orchestrates a pause between seasons.
Indifferent to families now,
Birds criss-cross in flight,
Rising up from a shabby vegetable patch,
From the plumes of iron-weed;
Becoming tidal, relating again to the stars;
Waiting for the light to change over the hemisphere;
For themselves to become a cloud of meteors.

And Yet

Today feels like forever, and yet,
The gold striped wasp seems lean and overworked;
A backwoods mother with her wood not in
And the kerosene can almost empty.
She crawls over the split logs this way, that way.
She is distracted. But how still the leaves lie,
Drooping with inertia. The thick green has drained away.
Transparent now, red and yellow, they lie
On the air, languid, ready to let go. And yet,
The chickadee works his throat in the red pines,
Insisting on territory and a background of insects
Sings to fertility the hum of everlasting hope.
Here in the center of the forest the hot sun
Comes into the clearing. Soon it will snow.

VI

Rhythm

I am the drummer's daughter.
He beat time out of me.
Rat-a-tat-tat
Rat-a-tat-tat
In Norfolk on the sea.
Young he was and handsome.
A gambler, by G.
I was his first-born daughter.
He rolled the dice for me.
And down I dropped ripe as a plum
Out of my mama's belly.

Young he was and handsome
And he lived carelessly.
The sailors rolled him over
And took his green money.
My mama sewed his pockets up
But it didn't work, by G.
We were poor, my mama and I,
In Norfolk on the sea.
Boom, boom, rat-a-tat-tat
Down dropped another little brat
Out of my mama's belly.

I hardly saw my daddy,
His music set him free.
He slept in my mama's great big bed
And he smelled of strong whiskey.
My mama laughed and scolded
Happy as she could be.
Boom, boom, rat-a-tat-tat
Down dropped another little brat
Out of my mama's belly.

My daddy's dust is scattered.
My mama's salt as the sea.

And when I'm ready to lay me down
Here's what they'll say of me.
She is a drummer's daughter.
She learned what her daddy taught her.
Never to drink cold water
And to keep her pockets free.
To beat time out of her heart
Or she must lose at the start
For, if she's a drummer's daughter,
She'll have to beat time, by G.

Being a Woman

You can talk to yourself all you want to.
After all, you were the only one who ever heard
What you were saying. And even you forgot
Those brilliant flashes seen from afar, like Toledo
Brooding, burning up from the Moorish scimitar.

Sunk in umber, illuminated at the edges by fitful lightning,
You subside in the suburbs. Hidden in the shadow of hedges
You urge your dog to lift his leg on the neighbor's shrubs.

Soldiers are approaching. They are everywhere.
Behind the lamp-post the dog sends unknown messages
To the unknown. A sensible union of the senses.
The disengaged ego making its own patterns.
The voice of the urine saying this has washed away my salt,
My minerals. My kidneys bless you, defy you, invite you
To come out and yip with me in the schizophrenic night.

Cocks and Mares

Every man wants to be a stud.
His nature drives him.
Hanging between his legs
The heavy weight of scrotum.
He wants to bring forth God.
He wants God to come
Out of those common eggs.
But he can't tell his cock
From a rooster's. However,
I'm a horse, he says,
Prancing up and down.
What am I doing here
In the hen house?
Diddle you. Doodle doo.
In this fashion he goes on
Pretending that women are fowl
And that he is a stallion.
You can hear him crowing
When the wild mares
Come up out of the night fields
Whistling through their nostrils
In their rhythmic pounding,
In the sound of their deep breathing.

Shotgun Wedding

The bride is not yet married to the groom.
Caught in the last pose of a matron's dream,
She is a father's nightmare of illusion.
Trailing ribbons of gauzy particles,
The bridegroom's chariot
Exhorts the maidenly throngs
In fireworks, explosions!
They approach the zenith
Rowing the air like a pair of swans
With blood-red eyes.
In snowy plumage, restive,
With folded wings,
They tender themselves, ready to leap
And spread their fans to the showy entrances.
The musical anguish and anti-joy
Rumble in earth like thunder of fissures,
Warning too late
Of the descent
Into the anxious fingers and mouths
Of the hungry tribe.

Whose Scene?

I crawl up the couch leg feeling
Your blond hair, your bloomy skin.
What do I want from you, giant?
I am afraid. But I laugh; I enjoy.
You fabricate. The words and music tremble
And thunder my thin blood.
The air is heated; odor of indian oil.
Trussed bed where bodies grapple; arms, legs,
Breasts, balls; the giants copulating.
I crawl up a wall and open my wings
And flutter down in borrowed ecstasy.

But then not open ended as it ought to be;
The beer, the refrigerator, the dull
Sequel shrinks to five rooms
In a treeless suburb. And cockroach that I am,
I go behind the baseboard to fornicate and spread
Myself, ancient as the ovulum and sperm.

Bringing the Babies

With no thatched roofs,
Our sky is not defined by faery birds;
Their stretched-out long ridiculous legs
Thin as sticks the wicked stepmother
Hid in her apron so she could
Beat the true daughter when it was time to dance.
Straws from their blowzy nests
(in the old arrangement)
Straggled down soot-filled chimneys
And sometimes caught fire,
Sucked up again with a rising draft
To flicker like altar candles.
In every grim fetus a memory
Folded as the naked stork in its egg:
Enormous white wings slowly clapping overhead,
Hauled by some mid-wife of the wind.

Who's Out?

In a moment
Grandmother will return.
The glazed shepherdess expects her,
The marble table.

Behind paneled doors
Our aunts laugh with authority;
Lean forward from their waists,
Have well-proportioned chins
And busy feet.

Grandmother's chin quivers
When she reads the book review
For Monday Club.

When eighty-eight, grandfather puts on his hat
And exits from the porch
Naked as a plucked rooster.

Aunt Dodo ferrets in the boot closet
And lashes us to straight chairs
Under lavender leaded windows
Where we sit for fifty years
Doing our best.

Grandfather reappears pointing to a dish
Of cooked raisins and says,
"It was Chautauqua
Got the woman out of the kitchen."

Family

We left, repeating, "love . . . care."
The heaviness of bodies close;
Imbalance.
You were waiting until we were gone
To put back the records;
Vacuum.
We ate too much food;
Drank coffee, tea, beer.
It was difficult to fit
Into the uncomfortable chairs;
To sit waiting for something
To come to pass. Doorways
Were not in our heads.
We were too heavy to be inside
Denting and sagging the calendar.
You brought in the corpse to show
Its bloody stumps,
And killed it again out of boredom.
It stared without any memory,
Without arms or face.
It was all we had to kiss good-by.

In No Time

Agitated for many hours I read both the news
And the life of the mayfly.
The cheap electric clock ran like a blood bank
Full of irregularities.
In no time the floor was carpeted with boxes of old poems.
These were abortions that I could not love.
One cat fought the other and the dogs lay among the notebooks
Not even earning their sleep.
This is a distant nest from the one my mother made,
And not only that,
My hair is not the way it was at all.

Mine

Sick at heart
I lie down
Among those who dream of murder.
While I am sleeping
They take away my blankets.
The sparrows fly up from the snow
And hunch in the bushes.
I walk slowly away, shivering.
I have died ahead of my body.
It drags behind me.
Come, they say, hiding their smiles,
Surely you can do something
About this bloody thing that is following you.
You know it is yours.

VII

Bored on a Greyhound

Settled in the seat
In front of instant lovers,
Their kisses sticky in my ears
Popping with altitude.
Semis line the roadside
Slogging back to Yuma.
Hands whispering *stop it*
Move restlessly,
Feeding on private giggles.
Jokes rise up inside their clothes,
Yawning.

En Route

Tractor trailers
Packed like killer whales
Around a roadside diner
In Tucumcari,
Belly in the spring snow squall.
Vacant-eyed,
Out of stranded Greyhounds,
We shuffle toward counters of leaky pies
And dingy goblets of Jello.
I read of old Chief Wautonamah,
Unfortunate Apache,
Lying on the mountain
Where our road goes,
Buried now, impassible.
How his daughter, Kari,
Leaped from a mesquite tree
To stab Tonapon
Because he had killed Tocom.
And then like Juliet,
She stabbed herself for love.
How old Wautonamah,
In the custom of legends,
Thrust her dagger
Into his own breast
Expiring upon their bodies,
Crying, "To-com-Kari!"
That is where we sit waiting
For the roads to be cleared.
In this diner on route sixty-six
In February.

Los Angeles

Going into the poison city we took a bus
To Japanese Town. Ladies,
Perhaps from Hiroshima, masked in white uniforms,
Served us. You ordered noodles and shrimp in Kumamoto dialect.
Chopsticks were packaged in art paper from Osaka.
The noodles slid in the bowl.
Using four paper napkins, I wiped my lips.
The scent of tea rose in delicate vapor.
Windows were framed with rice paper and bamboo.
We were considerate in shops where many small objects
Were inlaid with mother-of-pearl.
At the art company Mr. Tsuchiya showed us
Fine paintings on glass. Very rare.
Picking up your exquisite Sumi portfolio,
Oddly, the conversation with him did not concern frames
As much as certain excellent doctors.
Very obsequious.
The sun went down with a corona
Radiating like Van Gogh's last madness in the acid air.
We waited on Main Street for the bus.

The Infant

The sky is a fat belly
Blown up with gas,
With millions of belly buttons.

The sky is a head turned away,
With long gray hairs.
It is looking at God.

The sky is a voice speaking quietly.
Lonely, it drags up the spiders
Into its aching drifting whispers.

The sky is an eye; round, blind,
Milked over without any memory,
Pretending to be alert.

The sky is a pale fingernail;
The cold blue fingertip of an embryo
Still-born; laid out for the funeral.

Laguna Beach

The shingle roofs burgeon moss, green as tender acacia.
Under their eaves giant roses in cinemascope flash
Over-developed boobs; huge green penises rise, hairy,
Bristling with impotence, into trees that hold them.
Meanwhile the trees wait around on one foot for a place
To set the penises aside. It rains.
The sun draws off all the water.
Nature says yes to everything.

Saguaro

Buttoned up, nailed, exactly riveted ribs
Coming together at the top of the idiot head
With a bloom and pale shock of what might be hair.
Don't endanger yourself, but feel that green skin.
They're so human. The stubs at the ends
Of those beseeching arms with little fruits
Like maimed fingers. And the high whistle
Air makes rushing up those spines. You feel
That presently when they have grown more arms
They will be useful, do something, march in file.

Shadow

Streaks of dirty blue tape the Pacific together.
Yellow is rolling from shadow to shadow.
Like a proverb, the California gull
Hunches on black rock
Pointing a sullen profile.
Smear of oil; smell of dinosaurs.
Our lump hearts wait for the tremors.
Wet-suited surfers, modified plastic saviors,
Mount the waves and water-walk toward the golden city.

San Andreas Fault

Flat as copper sheeting,
Sun flushes up at noon.
Then the metallic disk is gone.
Under green swells the city undulates.
Adapted beasts of terraces
Gulp quietly. Along forgotten trenches cobalt glistens.
Eyes larger than before waver like lanterns;
Children of twilight moving about.
Submerged, rooms and caverns breathe;
Pouring darkness in and out of windows.
Passing unnoticed, far off, ethereal sounds of whales.
While carbon continues to sift like snow in the other world.

Out of Los Angeles

Coming into St. Louis, our heads still garbled
With Indian Spanish lilt and monotone.
The bus heavy with fumes and bodies.
We ride along the dry grass with herds of black Angus.
Demonic signs advise to gas up, have a Lark,
Get an exciting homesite in Eureka, save bucks on trucks.
Hounding, baying through diseased patches of elms,
Time's mobile sales and Black Madonna Shrine and grotto,
Going America's polluted trail by bus,
Nosing the smell from surf to surf,
Yipping with the dog day after day
On the track of the thief
Who rip-gutted mother earth, our angel mother;
Her belly slit from crotch to Oyster Bay.

VIII

The Sweeper
and the Sweeper's Son

There was an old lady lived on the fourth floor,
With a ral-dee-o and daughters four.
She spent her time tweezing her beard
For she feared their disgust at the sight of her weird
Chin whiskers. Oh, the pity.
She was hirsute and her eyes were bleared.
She cried all day behind her door, "What a bore!
Have mercy on four young girls in a wicked city."

But little she knew
That they kept in the flue
A sweeper's son who had eyes of blue;
Who went in and out like a stealthy screw
With a ral-dee-o and what could she do?
But she tweezed her beard and cried, "Oh, the pity
Of raising four daughters up in a wicked city."

By and by came the sweeper man,
A dirty old whiskered old sweep named Dan,
Shouting, "What! are you up in the chimney again?
What is it you're sweeping and sweeping out?"
With a ral-dee-o; oh, he was a bore.
Then he sees their mother behind the door.

It took some time to see who was with whom
But all has been tidied with handle and broom.
The four young ladies are locked in their room.
The sweeper's lad cries outside in the gloom,
"Ah, what a pity
To be a poor lad alone in a wicked city."

With a ral-dee-o up on the fourth floor
The old lady's dancing; she's crying no more

Saying, "La, my dear sir"; and, "old Dan"; and, "Sure
'Tis a pity to be a poor woman alone
On a night like this in the city."

Now ral-dee-o her whiskers grow
But she has no time for tweezing them. So
To tell old Dan from the old dame bore,
You must cleave them apart up on the fourth floor.
Their chin whiskers reach from the bed to the door.
That's all there is. There isn't any more.

How I Was Saved
from Dying of Hunger

(for William B. Goodman)

Off Phantom Town five fathoms down
Myself a fish did spy.
My sole, he was a flat fillet.
His one eye stared up through the bay.
"A chafing dish," cried I.

"Not so," he said in low reply,
"A sole in hellish grease must fry.
Or bake a sole in heavenly pie."
But here he faltered and grew shy,
And lo, an angel fish came by.
" 'Tis stern unbuttered," I did sigh,
"But make it a soufflé."

Thus musing, I fell overboard
And as I sank, the sole said, "Lord,
We thank you for this gourmet."

War with Words

Armature, that's what I need, cried the lady of doubtful charm.
Brood about that. There's a Teutonic stem there.
A hillock of a woman, with no heart,
Provoking discharge in the council-chamber.
To stretch, distend, distribute,
Depends upon practice and custom. The gusset resembles
The husk of a bean and also refers to that piece of mail
With which the arm hole is covered. Armature, cried the lady.
But she was not enchanted. Her song gaped open like a wound.
Be my protector, she continued. And after the carousal, the
   carminative.
Then let her choose her own scarp,
Perceiving as she will, her battlement,
And dwell or dwindle.

A Woman I Once Knew

Several set their traps for me
But I did as I pleased.
I broke my skinny ribs on bears,
I chafed their furry knees.

Grizzlies I hugged and fuzzy browns,
Mean-eyed and rough as pigs.
My, how the crepe de Chine wore down
What loved their blasted figs.

Bears dance and bears moan
And bears know how to strut.
And I'm a woman of the zoo
That knows them butt for butt.

Come and hear the lions scream
And tease the chimpanzee,
Peel your bananas, dirty louts,
And spit your luke-warm tea.

I've got a rock round cave of ice
And rugs with snarling jaws,
And when I winter through on fat
I hang my blouse on claws.

The Nose

Everyone complains about the nose.
If you notice, it is stuck to your face.
In the morning it will be red.
If you are a woman you can cover it with makeup.
If you are a man it means you had a good time last night.
Noses are phallic symbols.
So are fingers, monuments, trees, and cucumbers.
The familiar, "He knows his stuff," should be looked into.
This may be where the word "throes" originated.
There is big business in nose jobs,
The small nose having gained popularity during the Christian
    boom.
Noses get out of joint but a broken nose
Is never the same thing as a broken heart.
They say, "Bless your heart." "Shake hands." "Blow your nose."
When kissing there is apt to be a battle of wills
Over which side your nose will go on.
While a nose bleed, next to a good cry, is a natural physic;
A nosey person smells you out and looking down your nose
Will make you cross-eyed.
Although the nose is no longer used for rooting and shoving,
It still gets into some unlikely places.
The old sayings: He won by a nose, and,
He cut off his nose to spite his face,
Illustrate the value of the nose.
In conclusion, three out of four children
Are still equipped with noses at birth;
And the nose, more often than not,
Accompanies the body to its last resting place.

The Vain Poet Lectures
at a High School in Arizona

He told them about himself;
How it was to be married to his wife.
"A poet has sensibility," he said.
He read his poem about love.
He walked up and down
With his thumb in his studded belt.
They snickered and he smiled.
"What do you mean by laid?"
The student with pink pimples asked.
He smiled even more broadly,
"Just that," he said.
The room tilted up
Into his winking look.
"Do your own thing,"
He said. "Make a noise.
Make yourselves heard."
He brushed his hand over his head.
"What do you think of poets?"
He said, "Are they real people?"
The purple sweaters, white blouses,
Bluejeans; the cropped hair,
The long blond tresses,
The cowboy boots, the short dresses;
The blue eyes, the brown eyes;
The dark Indian faces: all
Got up when the bell rang
And moved like stampeding cattle
Toward the hall.

Lesson

In the days when his mind was simple,
Before he learned the rules,
Sam A. was a pupil
In the orchards of the people.
He went to school.
Dense rhetoric and physics
And beards to hide the fools;
Napalm and pears and peaches
And marvelous cutting tools;
Ways and means, the National Guard,
And saffron submarines.

He leaned beyond his body
On an uncharted course.
Hairy and sick and sweating,
He earned the mind's inverse.
And bitter in his hide
With speed and speed and worse;
With oily glands and scales;
He lay on the floors and cried
In Madison's crowded jails.

In the days when his mind was simple,
Before he learned the rules,
Sam A. was a poet
In the orchards of the people.
And his agony was to know it,
Among the clean-shaven fools.
Napalm and pears and peaches,
We learn what the pupil teaches:
That the mind is the body's curse.
With his simian arm that reaches
Out to the universe.

Lesson for Parents

Oh save the blue and gluttonous babe,
Who from his diaper took the pin
And thrust it in his epiglottis.
Abraham. We called him Abe.
Sir, his life was without sin.
A trenchant lesson he has taught us.
Nor will we forget this day
That infant taste cannot be trusted.
From his milk he turned away.
While the pin he ate was rusted.

IX

Wavering

What makes you think you're so different?
That was my weaker self hanging around outside the door.
The voices over the telephone were accusing, too.
"Must you always be you?" (They had the advantage,
More bold without faces. They swirled a few icecubes
With a suggestive pause.) For a moment
I took my heart out and held it in my hands.
Then I put it back. This is how it is in a competitive world.
But, I will not eat my own heart. I will not.

Survival

Miss Wilma Buttle,
Who did not die
For five years
While suffering
Leukemia,
Was thick and florid,
Uncomfortably fierce.
It wasn't until she
Admitted that no one,
Not even her mother,
Cared . . . Her expression
Was like a lizard's;
Eyes deep in armor.
She, herself, often forgot
To take her medicine.
She got her graduate degree
After a series of treatments
And went to teach
Near a hospital.
She carried a card
Which told of her condition.
All the others
Who started out with her
In that group that was given
Not much hope, but,
So much laboratory,
All the others died.
She spoke of them objectively.
Her sister, she said,
Had not been fond of her.

Osmosis

If I decide it is better to be me than you
I will need to discount that your hair is thick and long,
At the same time knowing that some who are not yet born
Will die early and pitiful. Out of blue eyes
Bluer than any strange gray blue I have ever seen
You look back at me, your bluejeans the same
Faded cloth everywhere walking away from me.
I am torn out of myself thinking it is better
To be this moment aching that I am
Also being you remembering me now.

Passengers

Deep in my skull, in the wormy cranium,
The long segments of history ooze.
I know that the old, the infirm, the laggards must stay
Behind when you leave on your silver ships
Never to return. There your eyes are going through me to the stars.
Yes, I applied . . . prehensile arms, rudimentary hair,
Swiveled neck (as yours). My eyes bore
Into the Pleiades; probed the wound that was always there. Was
  there
When I dangled from the cord. Yes, I came
Hanging, swinging like something to be catapulted
Out. My aborted flying. The heavy package
Is all that remains; the folds
Relaxed and the pod with its beautiful limbs distorted.

Monologue from
Mahogany Row

The purple nose spoke to the leader of the cotillion.
I am a square chin, it said.
Do your best, the supervisor advised. De-image yourself.
De-emphasize expenses. Cut costs.
Right arm to the left leg goes,
Swing your partner by the hose.
Are you a virgin, dear old widow?
By trying hard and confessing to your subhuman fantasies,
You may titillate this limp thing.
But be careful. Someone might peek.
Hello. Hello. This is me.
Did you hear the phone ring?
Ah, we were poor. I, of course,
Was working my heart out trying to make it.
You were out there thrashing in the bushes.
I'm a dull tool. Just a willing jock
To my supervisor. Tell me, super-duper,
Did I or didn't I work twenty-six hours yesterday?
God, let's not quarrel. Our quarrels were all over money.
You wanted toothpaste. I told you salt was good enough,
You extravagant beauty. My second wife listens to me.
When she doesn't I go up and play with my radio station.
I am a ham calling other hams. And while I'm up there,
Of course, I butcher my own meat.

Window Through Scratched Reading Glasses

You see through scratched reading glasses
That the ambulance has screamed around a corner
And a chihuahua is barking at the curb.
A woman in a peignoir runs out to get the chihuahua.
A man in a Volvo is ready to drive away.
The dog, tensed, playing a desperate game, dances out of reach.
After several false starts the man heaves out of the Volvo
And goes back toward one of the attached houses in the courtyard.
The dog and the woman follow him. A door slams.
Several pages of *Anna Karenina* later, when you look out again,
The Volvo is still at the curb.

Bazook

My aunt from St. Louis
Lost her husband,
So yesterday I invited her
And Dorothy to lunch.
Over in Dorothy's neighborhood
There was this couple
She used to think so much of—
Fred and Ida.
They had a lovely little house.
For two years all that two talked
Was, wait till we get to Florida,
Wait till we get to Florida.
It's going to be this and that.
Then finally they sold
And moved to Clearwater, Fla.
And built this place.
And the next thing we hear,
The wife's went bazook!
There they were in Clearwater
With this nice little place.
It got so bad Fred finally
Had her committed.
She didn't know him.
He was like a stranger.
He'd go to see her now and again.
But she was like a stranger.
He'd say, "Ida,"
And she wouldn't acknowledge.
He'd say, "It's Fred, Ida."
And the other day
We hear she died.
Now they're coming up to Tuscola
Where she was raised
To have the funeral,
And we're all going over there
To see them.

Something Deeper

I am still at the same subject—
Shredding facts—
As old women nervously
Pull apart
Whatever is put in their fingers;
Undoing all the years
Of mending, putting together;
Taking it apart now
In a stubborn reversal;
Tearing the milky curtain,
After something deeper
That did not occur
In all the time of making
And preparing.

X

The Song of Absinthe Granny

Among some hills there dwelt in parody
A young woman; me.
I was that gone with child
That before I knew it I had three
And they hung whining and twisting.
Why I wasn't more than thirty-nine
And sparse as a runt fruit tree.
Three pips that plagued the life out of me.
Ah me. It wore me down,
The grubs, the grubbing.
We were two inches thick in dust
For lack of scrubbing.
Diapers and panty-shirts and yolk of eggs.
One day in the mirror I saw my stringy legs
And I looked around
And saw string on the floor,
And string on the chair
And heads like wasps' nests
Full of stringy hair.
"Well," I said, "if you have string, knit.
Knit something, don't just sit."
We had the orchard drops,
But they didn't keep.
The milk came in bottles.
It came until the bottles were that deep
We fell over the bottles.
The milk dried on the floor.
"Drink it up," cried their papa,
And they all began to roar, "More!"
Well, time went on,
Not a bone that wasn't frayed.
Every chit was knicked and bit,
And nothing was paid.
We had the dog spayed.
"It looks like a lifetime,"
Their papa said.

"It's a good life, it's a good wife,
It's a good bed."
So I got the rifle out
To shoot him through the head.
But he went on smiling and sitting
And I looked around for a piece of string
To do some knitting.
Then I picked at the tiling
And the house fell down.
"Now you've done it," he said.
"I'm going to town.
Get them up out of there,
Put them to bed."
"I'm afraid to look," I whimpered,
"They might be dead."
"We're here, mama, under the shed."
Well, the winters wore on.
We had cats that hung around.
When I fed them they scratched.
How the little nippers loved them.
Cats and brats.
I couldn't see for my head was thatched
But they kept coming in when the door unlatched.
"I'll shave my head," I promised,
"I'll clip my mop.
This caterwauling has got to stop."
Well, all that's finished,
It's all been done.
Those were high kick summers,
It was bald galled fun.
Now the daft time's over
And the string is spun.
I'm all alone
To cull and be furry.
Not an extra page in the spanking story.
The wet britches dried

And the teeth came in.
The last one cried
And no new began.
Those were long hot summers,
Now the sun won't tarry.
My birds have flocked,
And I'm old and wary.
I'm old and worn and a cunning sipper,
And I'll outlive every little nipper.
And with what's left I'm chary,
And with what's left I'm chary.